The Healer's Diary

Poems

Nineteen poems in the "fruit" section: *Orange, Apple, Tangerine, Pomegranate, Papaya, Watermelon, Honeydew, Buddha's Hand, Cherry, Peach, Pear, Plum, Olive, Grapes, Wild Strawberry, Prune, Coconut, Banana, Raspberry* were published by LaNana Creek Press, Nacogdoches, Texas, in 2011 with artists Elizabeth Akamatzu, Piero Fenci and Charles Jones as a limited edition illustrated letterpress book under the title, *Growing Paradise*.

Bear Medicine and *War Mother* (under the title *Navajo Mother*) were previously published in the online journal, *Ekleksografia* #4, January 2011, a project of Ahadada Books.

Raspberry was previously published as *The Inexplicable* in the *Santa Fe Literary Review*, 2008.

Healing was previously published in the We'Moon Calendar 2000 and re-published, *In the Spirit of We'Moon: Celebrating 30 Years*, Mother Tongue Ink, 2011.

An earlier draft of *Papaya* was previously published under the title *Brazilian Cloud Forest* in *Urban Spaghetti*, #3, 2000.

An earlier draft of *Watermelon* was previously published under the title *Zuñi Pueblo* in a literary publication of Antioch College edited by Nova Ren Suma, 1996.

The
Healer's Diary

Poems

Ann Filemyr

SUNSTONE
PRESS

SANTA FE

Sunstone books may be purchased for educational, business,
or sales promotional use. For information please write:
Special Markets Department, Sunstone Press,
P.O. Box 2321, Santa Fe, New Mexico 87504-2321.

Book and Cover design › Vicki Ahl
Body typeface › Book Antiqua
Printed on acid free paper
⊗

Library of Congress Cataloging-in-Publication Data

Filemyr, Ann, 1958-
The healer's diary : poems / by Ann Filemyr.
p. cm.
ISBN 978-0-86534-853-0 (softcover : alk. paper)
I. Title.
PS3606.I385H43 2012
811'.6--dc23

                                    2011047596

WWW.SUNSTONEPRESS.COM
SUNSTONE PRESS / POST OFFICE BOX 2321 / SANTA FE, NM 87504-2321 /USA
(505) 988-4418 / ORDERS ONLY (800) 243-5644 / FAX (505) 988-1025

The creativity and tenacity of remarkable women
have inspired me: beloved Ondé Chymes,
my mother Sara Ann Walker Filemyr
and Keewaydinoquay, *mashkikikwe* and teacher.
Thank you.

Contents

1

11

111

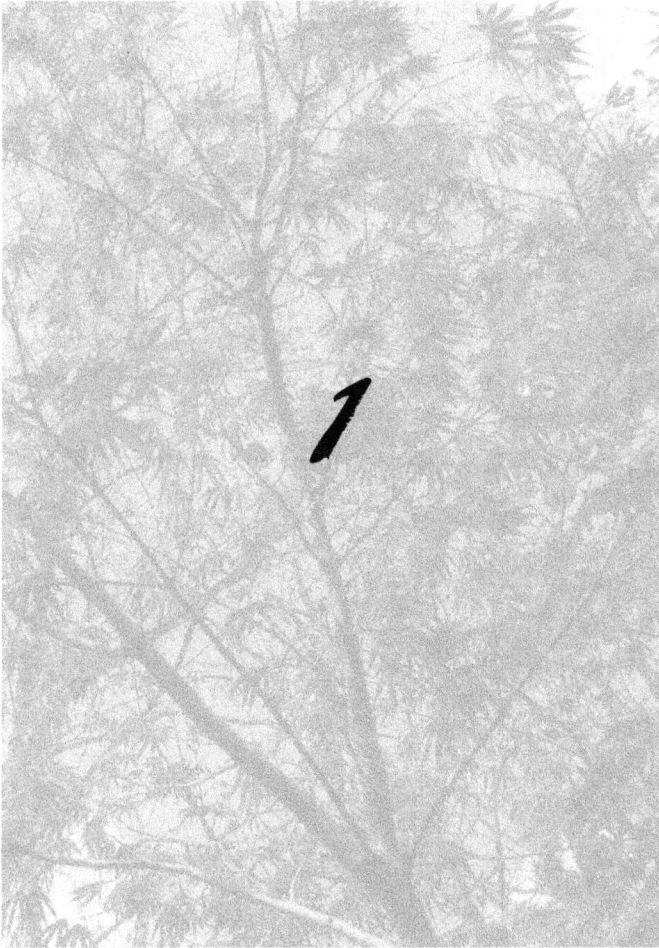

1

Orange

We had the shore at our backs and enormous stone Jesus
his arms outstretched pulling at the taffy clouds
salt spray, boardwalk, men lurking beneath
the rotted pilings, their private things
poking at the sky, and Joanie's Mom
with her dark Italian eyes and blond husband
calling me butterball, my chubby pink hand
reaching for an orange in their glass bowl.
They were the rich neighbors with fresh fruit
not neon sludge in aluminum can,
but round and bright, the way a tree made it,
and Joanie's thumb biting into its bottom
with those painted red nails like tiny swords
peeling that fragrant Florida in a long spiral
undressing the succulent fruit, juice on her fingers
she pulled off each lingering white thread,
I opened my mouth like a baby bird
to let her feed me, explosion in my mouth
the color of hummingbird gods,
my blue-eyed cat with the rumbling purr
warm beside me in bed as I peel
my Christmas stocking orange
sparks flaring up into the night
with each stroke of my hand
the way I am
always hungry

Apple

Sunlight hauled in by the muscle of leaves
beside a woman with her arms
curved around her swollen belly
yearning for a red-skinned fruit
warm and holy as a nest with spring eggs,
and yes, there was a man, or a rumor of a man
with bitter black seeds in his vest pocket
the Johnny apple man, kneeling
in muddy earth along the Olentangy
pushing in a handful with a twig prayer
for the hard cider pioneers, Westward ho!
My great-grandmother beneath a bonnet
cursing the heat in the back of a Calistoga
while her brothers ride prancing ponies in the prairie grass,
and yes, it was said in my childhood
that a serpent crouched in the crotch of two limbs
because sex was not perfect in the eye of god
but when he was not looking
she took a delicious bite
and the blessed hungry
reaching for sweetness in the green orchard
gave birth to knowledge

Plum

Making out in the convent orchard
ducking when shriveled nuns with gnarled hands
trimmed their trees into fruitfulness:
yellow plum, red plum, purple plum,
while giggling in mittens behind snow drifts
we throw back our heads to drink
slivovitch straight from the bottle.
Lisa the Catholic, Ellen the Jew
and me the Quaker crowd into the confessional
in the forgotten monastery of St. Gregory of Nazianz
to light up. Later we share a six-pack in the tomb
of Ambrose Oswald, the occult founder
of a nineteenth century German sect of believers
who hid out in this beech forest to build their private empire.
At midnight between the crosses of buried brothers
we toast our dead debating the power of war
to make immigrants out of farmers
because everyone we are descended from
fled from somewhere sometime ago.
Reading Virginia Woolf, Gertrude Stein,
living off bazooka bubble gum, shots
of tequila, salt on the hump of a thumb,
dead worm spinning the bottle,
fox-trotting around campus
our mouths wide open to taste
the electric air before lightning strike

Tangerine

Walking home from the bus stop
past paper bunnies and painted eggs
taped to the dollar store window
past the tavern drunks spewing
cigarette smoke, the belch of traffic,
Friday night fish fry bar bands playing polka
stumbling through the slush
of late winter melt
on Milwaukee's lower eastside
junkies' needles litter the gutter.
I look up into a sudden hush
Easter snow beginning to spin
dizzy in the halo of street light.
Like a kid I stick out my tongue
wanting one cold French kiss, someone to hold
in my torn black wool angel arms
right here on the corner by the Italian grocer
beside buckets of green olives, shelves of pasta
a pyramid of bright tangerines, but I am alone
and the boy I want
with his ponytail and leather jacket
does not come. At sixteen
I would have his baby.
I would marry him.
But I am too much
trouble. No man
can tame me.
That's what he said.

Pear

In a maple and beech forest
in the stairwell of a girls' dorm
in the kitchen of an old hotel
on a black rotary phone with a twisted cord
on the faded living room carpet of an old bungalow
on the forgotten sand dune of a melted glacier
in an abandoned farmhouse beside the Grand River
in a garden of broken abalone
in a burned down button factory
near the bend in the river
near an altar to Kali
near railroad tracks on the Westside
in a bathtub of Israeli salt
in an old sweater with frayed elbows
in a red silk slip
on the Moray Firth
on the fourth floor
on the fire escape
in an office with a single window
in the window of a closed café
in the doorway of a Hindu temple
behind a closed door
beside a dead elm
between stone walls
with a pear in her hand and pear in her mouth
with her pear hips and pear belly
with hope and fear and longing
in that place
she touches
the terrible mysterious thing
some call love

Grape

In that house of love with the tides
rising and falling away
treacherous rocks smoky with seaweed
and a ripple of purple crocus
beneath the awning each spring,
Love speaks in this language
with no beginning and no end
only we fail to name it as it marks us. We
forget the importance of the sea
why the dark undertow must pull
why day and night yield in turn
why the house has more than two stories
and why each story
has more than two rooms. Love like this
cluster of grapes, tender skin,
juice dripping from your chin, wine
in the fluted glass, my lips stained with yours.
No matter what else happens
inside these jumbled rooms, I felt it once
the love that cannot be broken. The lock
picked, door ajar, even if the window is rusted shut.
Harvest waiting in the vineyard
rows along California roads
brown hands bent to the task of baskets.
As we pass by I whisper, Thank you,
thank you for your labor. You see
love is what we want, the sensual humming
of the sea, its sweet heavy scent, the pulsing
rhythm of waves

Cherry

Oh little body, temple of desire
monks dancing beneath the cherry blossoms
Sakura in Kyoto, the rice wine merchant smiling
business boys in black suits drinking at noon
singing syllables in *kanji*. Later
at the zendo in New Mexico
hollering mantras, reciting riddle tricks,
teetering toward enlightenment
(war is a sledgehammer hitting smoke)
she tries eating her cherry heart
that taiko drum driving her hard
up this dirt road, wanting only the sun
that big holy fire, that round light
to mount her

Bowing to merciful Kuan Yin,
she paces slowly
wanting her lover's breast,
the full moon of it,
the stone weight of it,
salt beneath her robe
heat in the damp places
where flesh folds back against itself
and all are born. Here despite
mandatory silence
the echoing sage flowers
promiscuous as gravel

Buddha's Hand

With the next feathered breath
she admits she is
out in the cold dawn
god hunting

Papaya

We drive higher
leaving the twisting road
tires twitch as pavement gives way
to hand-hewn cobbles pounded into mud.
Brazilian cloud forest hugs the hungry sky midway
between Tierra del Fuego and Bahia. You turn
off the beetle's engine and we unfold like moths out of cocoons
to feel each drop of cloud swelling into dew
the glistening wet of each leaf, my skin licked clean
by this tongue of quivering mist

Clouds flooding fill the stone pools
between broken cliffs
before falling
falling
falling
for thousands of feet, for years
against rock, against clay
against the spindly roots of the mangrove
wave into ravenous wave
feeding the cavernous fold
where mountain tumbles into the sea

In the echoing *cascata,*
I hear the thundering avalanche of horse hooves,
I say, *Take me.* Blood pounding we hike
up the tangled trail made by holy men mad for God.
We stumble into their unfinished cathedral
claimed by vine-laden bromyliads
their sharp red tongues trilling
the green ears of the Earth.

Water pounds
the monk-chiseled cobblestones
as you peel papaya with the blade of your knife
slicing through the succulent orchid dusk
beak first, the brilliant
beija-flor wings into light

Grab me. Hold me.
Now I know how
flower becomes bird
cloud becomes ocean
the heart falling like water
invents paradise
in more than one language
at once

Banana

A thousand pink birds blow sideways,
plastic shopping bags tangling in the limbs
of half-dead boulevard trees
on the road into Dakar. I grip the wheel
weave past goats, chickens
zigzag between blaring horns,
small painted busses jingle with metal bells,
the radio warbles in French, Arabic, Wolof
a shrill cry from the minaret above the din
calls the faithful to morning prayer.
Men turn, kneel, bow their foreheads
to a distant black stone
in the brotherhood of belonging.
I follow the women
walking to the *fibre marche*
each one in her *grand bu-bu*
gliding past me as I loop
looking for a space to park
between a wagon with two mules
and a Mercedes coup.
Jostling into the hectare of tiny stalls
violet, amber, cinnamon
ivory, diamond, royal blue
shimmering turquoise
drunk from the sheer volume of color
I am pushed forward into the maze
until unable to move
I step into one stall and sigh.
A Fulani child, not yet scarred
with the ritual beauty mark,
pleads in a soft voice,
reaches out to finger

an exquisite gold-edged purple
plantain, her mother slaps her hand
pulls her away. I too have hungered
for the beautiful things
my mother could not
give me: a banana picked ripe.

Coconut

Standing on the upper deck of the ferry
leaving Mindelo for the outer island,
Cape Verde, sharp volcanic rock,
date palms waving their giant fronds as we
head out into open sea. Flying fish leap and drop
into the sputtering azure. Crates of coconuts
rock as the little boat leaps and lurches. The sea wind
blows tangles into the thick black hair of a girl
on the verge of womanhood
longing for the swift machete of love
to sever her dark shell and let spill
all she is

Pomegranate

Listen to it: the word, amorous, voluptuous vowels
ending with the hiss of a rattelesnake
a word that makes my skin ache,
I feel torrential, oceanic, blazing,
strong as the bent elbow
of a tango dancer, ready
to swing between head
and rose-colored cunt.
I have to leave you now, mother,
go below into the flaming dark,
sink into the mud beneath waves,
down into that deep unknown
where only I can be,
for I have taken the fruit
peeled back the rough bark
exposing the ruby flesh
surrounding each dark seed.
I have to give myself away.
You understand. You were a girl once.
The path in is hidden,
but I will find it.

I am the fruit.
Break me open.
Take me whole.

Prune

She decided to stop eating. First the smell of meat made her nauseas. Then all food became filth to her. We tried feeding her chocolate ice cream, banana split, a peach, anything. She turned away from us. We watched her flesh fall away, her eyes sink, her bones jut out, her clothes balloon around her. She slung low jeans around protruding hips smiling in the mirror when we were not looking.

We begged her to eat. We cried. We cajoled. We teased her twigginess. Finally she brought a bag full of dark shriveled fruit into our dorm room on the fourth floor.

Maybe one prune per day, she said.

Fascinated we watched as her gleaming white front teeth pulled the shriveled skin away from the tender dried plum. She chewed that single bite twenty times. Then almost unable to swallow, she fought her gagging reflex to get it down. We saw the lump of chewed skin work its way down her neck into her throat. Then she took one tiny sip of water and wiped her mouth with the back of her hand.

She grimaced telling us, *That's enough. I can't eat anymore.* And threw the rest of the prune into the trash.

We became so afraid that we huddled around the pay phone at the end of the hall pumping dimes into its slot to tell her mother. Exasperated her mother cried out, *What can I do? My baby won't eat!*

We knew then that her mother was powerless. We hung up the phone understanding that her rebellion was directed at her mother's round hips, her full breasts, her complicated muddy female life. We began to appear plump as pears, hideous fleshy girls with ample growing curves, doomed to blood and babies.

She made us nervous. We could not decide whether to diet or fatten up. If we broke open a candy bar in front of her, she turned up her nose and walked away. How could we persuade her to eat and live? We watched as she disappeared into a hollow-eyed, smart-mouthed skeleton.

We learned the word for it: anorexia. We read the articles citing statistics of teenagers bombarded by beauty myths choosing to deny the animal impulse to eat. We despised fashion models, tearing up images of size 2 girls parading around in haute couture. We scorched slick pages of Vogue and Cosmo with cheap lighters, left them in the ashtray to smolder.

We tried to tell her how beautiful she was before. She sneered at our pitiful ugliness. She despised our bulging breasts, the lump of our hips, the small mound below our belly buttons softening in our monthly cycles. We sucked in our stomachs when she walked past.

She was fierce, our friend, and we began to fear her. She could control the urge to feed herself. She could stop the world. She could keep her monthly blood from flowing. She had become thin and flat as a piece of paper. The wind ate her. She was no more one of us. We could no longer know her.

Raspberry

Who can name the tart, ripe flesh of the inexplicable?
Startled by the reverberating whirr of hummingbird wings
the honeybee kneels deeper in Sacred datura; my sister's
son drops a blue marble in a blue lake beneath blue
clouds; the summer wind flowers in the yellow
pollen heat, and I write wondering whether
the Peace Studies professor will awaken from his coma,
the landscape painter will lose her sight, will waves
erode a distant shore? I have seen how light falls,
how tides rise, how the sky throws shadows down.
At thirteen we lied to strangers
threw stolen cash across a bar
got drunk and hitch-hiked back roads
dangerous and endangered
as our father studied sundogs
concluding that the endless horizon
curved above him like the body of his mistress
while our mother made raspberry jam
from the patch behind the barn.
No one knows why
I write my heart
wondering how to be
female about it
and just state life
for what it is

Peach

Near the cliff dwellings in Frijoles Canyon
where the Cochiti lived before Spaniards brought peaches
in the time before she knew what she wanted
she changes
                        water to blood to milk
for the fertile moon has already touched her
and the stream of all that being
flows in the dark head of wild amaranth
volcanic ash
                        the wide-legged squat
of an ancestor near a stone lion.
She is not ready. She is too young.
It is too late. The father has gone
                        leaving his seed.
What is this incredible sweet flesh
This tenderness? This delight?
                        We make it ours
in the verb and tongue
of that doing, for she is now
                        bent to birth
breathing every shade of light
                        pulling
from the heart's dark passage
                        as peach trees
flowering all around her
                        push life

Watermelon

Not the first time at Zuni
I fill your cup with watermelon
stretch out against the green cloth
watching clouds billow up
rain-blue but quiet. Listen,
you can hear the clowns
making everybody laugh
as Katsina dancers in rain masks gather
for their entrance to the plaza
as adobe bread ovens bake
moon-shaped loaves for the feast
as rez dawgs lap the shadows
as each one here

waits for the wind
to shoulder its thunderous snake
the fierce afternoon wind
flicking its bright tongue at the mesa top
the wind that flees the Pacific
dropping the seedcorn of harvest
into the dreaming gardens of *Halona:wa*
the wind the ancestors ride
wearing a handwoven cloth of cloudlight
the pilgrimage wind on its silver journey
bringing summer monsoon
to the high red desert
like a song rising in our throats
until rain falls like the blue corn
the dancers dance for

We stumble, we strangers
guests of the dirt plaza
knowing nothing can change
the sweet taste of the red heart
in the black-seeded fruit of summer

Olive

Yesterday I met the old men of the Adriatic Sea
ankle deep in wavelets
blue trunks loose, hips stiff
sitting on metal benches against the cement wall.
They called to me as I swam deeper into the cold clear
salt of Croatia, they sang to me
of olives, the red wine
of Dalmatia, gray snakes slithering up dust
roads; they sang of sirens, grenades, hand guns, fighting
the force of Belgrade,
hiding their Serb wives
the brown-eyed mothers of their children who did not
sleep waiting in blood anger beneath the eclipsed moon
for war to end.
And they sang to me
of sweet calamari, the fragrant lavender on Hvar,
their bold sons parading as Roman soldiers at the ruins
posing for kuna
at Dioclesian's door.
Japanese tourists roll into Split by the busload
before sailing out to Brac or to Vis
islands like jewels in the ragged coast.

Wild Strawberry

I am going back to Ohio
to see redbuds bloom, the forest
floor covered with phlox,
gray sky hanging down
as the river flows over its banks
staining the cornfields with brown pools

I am going back to visit that place of rust and ruin
solvents poured out the backdoor of a bomb factory
crumbling asbestos, lead paint peeling
friends struggling with cancer. When I gathered
so much environmental health data
that no one wanted to hear
finally I had to leave. The one thing
I learned stumbling over the broken brick wall
of an abandoned paper mill
to pause beside the cracked dam
where the creek sings as it falls
is how persistently spring returns
even after ice breaks the branches
of century-old maples, and the pump dies
and the furnace won't work, just outside
mouse-ear chickweed opens beside jonquils
wolf spiders as big as my hand leap,
and one April walking beneath a stand of dead oak
I found a turtle working its way up out of red mud.

June comes along the edge of fallow fields
peppering the green with tiny red hearts
wild strawberries sweeter than sugar.
Popping one after another on my tongue,
I realize we die or survive. Spring comes.
I am going back to see it once again.

Honeydew

Can we change the ways we live and work so as to establish a
preserving harmony between the made and given worlds?
                                        – Wendell Berry

Oh made world, oh given world
oh world of grief, world of wounds

Given are the hours of sunlight
the cloud shedding rain
stars dropping tails of dust
eons of ocean laying down
lime upon clay upon sand.
Buried in the old delta, I find
a thumbnail-sized brachiopod,
small ancient seashell,
what other million year old being
could claim my heart?

On that May day
when I was supposed to be
black robe solemn pomp
graduating with my master's degree
I was instead on my hands and knees
tearing grass out of the lawn.
Raking spindly roots
through an old window screen
loosening soil to make a garden
in my city yard, imagining
pole beans, sweet peas, honeydew
melon that melts in the mouth
an orange bowl of acorn squash
tomato ripening beneath the dark leaf
beet fattening beneath my feet.

Making from what is given
food for the hungry

11

War Mother

for A.B.

Limping between the dead
a Navajo infantry soldier listens
to old school on ear plug
sweating ice, dust drying
in the blood of his split lip
leg twisted, boot dragging
in Afghani mud, the same
brick clay as back home;
thinking of his dad in Chinle
his mother at the stove
her back to him when he told her
the way her shoulders sagged
the wingbones jutting out
beneath her thin sweater
like a hummingbird folded into itself
that pause one pulse
before flight

three thousand years ago
built by masons without mortar
stone upon stone fitting together
tighter than sock, glove, bra, girdle
like skin over bone
no break, no seam, no thread
not even the rain penetrates
the white horse, her milk thistle nipples
breathing in the center room
when winter dawn breaks
casting its dagger of light
seventeen minutes
blinding

snow, raven in the rooming house
tangled barbwire trash
twisted plastic caught
kill the pain, grab the rattle
black song stops in the rasping throat
another young vet gone
cat collar in the owl nest
coyote tracking the lost pup

His mother wants to remember how
to sing beside the cactus

Virgin Mother, Feast Day, Taos

Consider beehive, ladder, window, door
toe hold, hand hold
coming down the canyon wall;
consider these places they walked
inhaling the sun-shot air,
moving between piñon,
in the long ago before horses
or tractors or traders or coins;
consider a child forced to kneel
before a statue of a half naked man
blood dripping from his sides
palms of his hands nailed, feet dangling,
bright spikes emanate from his haloed head,
consider that monster of compassion,
the savior of killers; now consider
flute players, drummers,
parrots with turquoise feathers,
two wheels of light looping across the sky;
consider the virgin mother draped in white cloth
carried through the crowd on Christmas Eve
beneath billowing clouds of fire
sparks shooting from raised rifles
dancers singing Tewa, not Spanish nor English,
in the Village Plaza. Consider how
she bled, labored, opened her legs
a son was born. In his name came horror
he could not predict. Consider the bronze body
of the vicious bishop
lording over the town square.
Consider also grains of corn pollen
finer than silk
gathered for prayer
by the holy man's attentive hands.
Consider this
when you open your mouth to feast.

Epiphany

It's the same woman
naked, upright, who came
in the wet grasses of dawn
the man's hands on her hips
moaning before the moon set;
the snake knew the polish
of oval egg in yellow nest,
knew the urge to live
never dies, offered this
single insight; she gasped
to see the oracle undulate
legless and free
she gazed into its milky eye
noticed the hairline split
and watched the serpent inch out
leaving behind what it was
shining in late summer sun.
The bead of sweat on her upper lip
tasted of salt, she trembled
as she reached out to touch
the pale empty shell
holding only the memory
of what it was, and knew then
what every living thing is
the moment before it is not.
When he returned she was
speechless and free
holding a snake skin in one hand
an apple in the other.
My father took the fruit and was fed.

Teen Mother, Rio Grande

Six months pregnant and stripping
off her summer dress
behind tamarack-colored willow
she dives into soundlessness.
The river's pulse racing
its taut muscle pulling her down.
Holding the blue sky in her breath
like a fish snaking rugged terrain
in the long haul from gorge to bosque
like sandhill crane beating back
the sure route to extinction
by bearing the next generation.
Despite statistics
she will survive
tougher, bolder
than before
in this realm beneath
the raging sun
another mother's story
begins

Mother on the Run

Red-speckled howl, swamp diary, capsized
in the holy spit of late afternoon rain
horse trader, train robber, disguised
in black paint, bearded, bent over,
sneaking upriver, enslaved
whipped by wind and children hollering
discarded in the dark, interrupted
by headlines, anonymous and unruly
I admire you, your instinct to survive
your dirty hands, your wide shoulders
your stories, the weight you carry each day
you get up, feed your children
still alive and unafraid to speak your name.

Rattle

My bones, the teeth in my head, the sockets of my eyes
the shape of the back of my skull, the dull
ache when I think of you, my brown son,
behind razor wire, riflemen poised in the tower.
How dare the arrogant
with their dirty secrets
punish you for being a man.
I shake my rattle at the sky and cry
shame on this settler slave nation
we both live in

Creed

for Meridel LeSeuer

It is so unpopular to be a pacifist
when the nation is at war.
Poor patriot who believes in peace.
How hard to hold firm
to the belief
that no mother births the enemy;
even the boy on that city street
who grabbed my purse on payday
and threw his fist in my face
when I refused to let go
he, too, is a poor woman's son.

Chaco Canyon

for E.A.

What if, at equinox
a dagger of light splits the spiral
as desire presses like a thumb
inside the tip of his cock
the child not yet conceived
becomes a million stars breaking
as she takes one step
falls hip deep into the brown rush
of the narrow canyon stream.
He reaches and pulls her
toward him, mud clinging to her thighs
and they continue the climb
to the thousand year old rock art
meteor etched in stone,
an animal with no name
racing across the galaxy.
Woman, man, they stand
beneath the ledge
looking up, how perfect
the evidence of that swift
night forever
her body will never
again be a girl's, her son
will want mama
to gaze with him
upon Orion's Belt
feeling his birth
from star dust

Working Mother

Seeing each client on the hour.
Ticking off email alerts with a painted fingernail.
Watching the hands on the clock rotate in synchronized procession.
Sucking the stale indoor air in the great machine of the familiar.
Doing another office tour of duty unable to answer the
the nagging question, how did you end up here
counting on biweekly paychecks to feed your family?
Blue suit. White blouse. Low heels. Fake pearls. Polite smile. Nod.
Juggle demand. Meet. Sit. Stand. Shake hand.
until the fist
rising in her chest
strikes fire

Child

Go to the gingko tree
I planted in the front yard
the year you were born.
Of course your umbilical cord
is wrapped around its root.
You are twins. I made it so.
Do you feel it now?
The ferocious yearning?
This is what it means to live.
Like the seed of the gingko
one day you will reveal your true sex
you too will flower, fruit and fall
in eighty-nine, or one hundred years.
Whenever you feel lost
stand beside this tree.
No one else knows
what you need.

Mother Tree

For two months we danced, moving in new ways, heels flexed, toes pointed, backs arched, hips swinging, bodies tumbling across the sprung floor. Then after the final Sunday matinee dance concert, we held hands and bowed, pleased with our choreography. Now what? We had no more reason to come together and sway.

Not yet ready to say good-bye, M. decides to take J. and me to her secret place on the river, to her Mother Tree. We scramble through weeds at the field edge, Queen Anne's lace, wild mustard, bedstraw, purple phlox, through broken stalks of last November's ploughed corn, until coming to an enormous five hundred year old sycamore. Saved from the logger's axe by its crooked trunk arching out over the river, reaching for sunlight in what would once have been thick, dark, deciduous forest. But all of that gone now, cut and milled for barns, dining room table and chairs, church with pulpit and polished pews, Cincinnati piano, maple dresser, china cabinet, the corner hutch for knick-knacks, axe handle, railroad tie, telegraph pole, plank road, every shop on Main street in the clapboard towns of the sprawling Midwest was made from this forest.

We clamber up the mother tree's back to watch the lazy brown river flow in the slippery twilight. J is in love with M, but I don't think M knows. J touches her hair, holds her eyes, says quiet things. Willowy M sighs, stretches out, agile as a lioness on a limb. *I come here,* she confesses, *to be away from my children, my man, the dog, the cats, everyone needs me to feed them.* She isn't complaining, it's just a fact. Here suspended above the shallow winding river her spine rests against the curved trunk of her mother tree and she listens to the water skimming over rock, watches the red-tailed hawk spinning in soundless air, and is lulled by the rising, falling, whisper of motion of the tree as it hangs nearly sideways from its dense weave of roots.

I notice the way the tree lurches out of the ground and how the soil slowly erodes from the mud bank. I do not say what I'am thinking. This tree will soon topple into the river becoming the beavers' home.

J quivers as near to M as she can get lying alongside her on the trunk. I am, of course, the furthest out, legs hanging down on either side of a sturdy branch, vivid chartreuse leaves unfurling around me. The spiked globes of last season's seed heads wobble in the spring breeze. Closing my eyes, I tilt my face toward the sun and do not look when I think I hear a kiss.

Milk

Thistle, nipple, joy tit,
suckling, mammal mother, whale,
cat with hungry kittens knocking her down
so they can guzzle the fine white floss of life,
first food. To thrive you must
open your mouth to what sustains,
hold joy close
for your task is to flourish.

Crescent Moon

Fingernail, shield, the white horns of breakfast croissants,
night flowering jasmine, the cat she let in
leaving beneath the early
moon. She lays a white sheet
beneath the Russian olive. If you
want the seed of a man to root
in your body, sleep beneath nothing
but the arc of moon dark and silver light
count the days between blood and heat
take what you want
to give away

Sacred Mother

Perhaps there persists
a memory of belonging we carry in the blood.
What happened to that ancient harmony?
The *auto-de-fe* and mercantilism
crashed together making
god = gold
and the pale frail ideal female
figment, shadow, soil
unattainable virgin distance
thirst for conquest
made men mad
afer the holyland was lost to infidels,
but Jew, Moslem, Catholic are brown-eyed cousins
snapping castanets to the pounding of flamenco heels,
Africa in it, of course, Africa in everything
in the rich fingering of Spanish guitar,
on the edge of salt sea, in our DNA the single shared
mother of everyone living today.
Think of it. Think of the
testosterone of the Pliocene
dinosaurs stomping around, and now
the feminization of frogs, estrogenic
sperm and the soft white sand
of the missile range. Where are you
Sacred Mother, tongue-tied
in the tangled web of your many
children. We are one
people, but we
do not yet
admit it.

Jemez Pueblo

Shivering in the January dark
we line the highway that snakes through the pueblo
waiting for dawn when the animals
dance down from the mountain
bringing flesh, fur, food, warmth
back to the people of the winter village.
Gust of cedar smoke erupts from the ridge top,
deer in turquoise masks paw the dust,
antelope race past single file,
three young buffalo dancers
shake their gourd rattles to keep beat
with the heart of the drum. Men sing.
Eagles prance. My low red belly empties
keeping rhythm with the other women here.
The oldest grandmothers of the pueblo
throw white corn to the frozen earth.
We scramble in the hard scrabble
to pocket one bright kernal
blessing us, each one of us
this cold dawn

111

Legacy

In their black and white wedding photo
his long nose, round glasses, bowtie;
her blonde hair twisted up
beneath a crown of babies breath
holding a bouquet of roses, smiling.
        My mother's Kansas
ranch parents: cattle, wheat, acres of prairie
when the horse bolted, her grandfather fell forward
onto the iron plow blade and bled to death on broken dirt.
        My grandparents left
the sod house, one room schoolhouse
summer of swarming locusts, a biblical famine,
left and never returned, the shadow of dust
billowing behind.
        My grandfather, the bug
scientist, helped develop DDT,
left a legacy of chemical poison,
but in his heart he believed
he was killing vermin to feed people.
        The cost of ignoring
how one thing becomes another:
aphid to robin's egg to fox,
kids running in the spray behind the mosquito-killing truck,
me and my brothers choking and laughing
in the smudged gray air.
        We who were
born to the poisoned world
have a legacy to heal.

It Began

by accident, like most things
horsing around after rehearsal
his cowboy boot hit my girlfriend in the eye
she screamed, gut instinct, I put my hands on her
drew it in, the hurt, my own eye blackened,
she was fine. After that I hid
my hands in my pockets.
No one taught me
the things I know.

Old Quaker Meeting House

London, 1978

I touch the worn wooden benches
rows of them, feel the palpable silence

think about the power of rebellion
they risked prison, chose exile

those who believed no man
stood between them and God

boarded the wooden ship
with simple things

leaving home and history

salt spray, horses below deck, the stench
red moon above heaving swells

when the creaking stinking ship
passed the treacherous shoals

and made its way upriver
from the shore scouts stared in disbelief

who were these shriveled pale people
who professed peace

stopping along the Delaware
where three centuries later I was born.

I sneak back across the Atlantic
curious about ancestors

headstone names erased by rain

British Isles

At twenty the immigrant girl went there where

family names lived in the cemetery, certainly, she

believed only that land's hands

could square her lost heart, should, would

openly embrace, face

the truth of her hurt, dirt

peasants who came before her.

Instead they spun her around, frowned,

Go home, the dead said,

learn who you are, far

away in the place of your birth, Earth.

I Was Her Helper

for Keewaydinoquay

I didn't want it
the responsibility, the pain
of other people's lives, enough
of my own, enough pain, but
that wasn't the point.

She needed a helper,
so I entered the stories
a hundred miles out
in cold freshwater sea,
sleepless nights
when the northern lights
danced to her drumbeat.
Learning to sing, I
memorized the multiple meanings
in a single scratch in birchbark
striving to know without fail
the green patterns
of that living forest.

I bent to the task, willing.

The Journey

Waiting for the bus with my backpack
heavy against my hips,
I flip my ticket to the driver, board,
swing my pack above my head.
An old man says, *Looks like you've done that before.*
Yes, crisscrossing Europe,
young and careless. City lights
blur in summer rain
the greyhound lumbers past the last
gas station before open road. I don't know
exactly where I'm going, but the old woman
said, *Come to my island and help*
me make medicines the people need.

Once in the time before time began
a female, part me and part mystery,
part animal and part fire
part human and part salt
ran upright, her bare toes splayed,
across the savannah and into the woods
with a baby at her breast. What she knew,
what she did, means we live.

I am going to go dig in the dirt
lift roots to sunlight and learn to pray.
I will bend my back over the mortar
take the pestle in my blistered hand.
This is the road I have taken to grind corn.

Copper Kettle

She gave me a copper kettle. Etched with the raw tip of her fingernail file in her floral, familiar handwriting she scraped these words onto its round metal belly:

Mishi Megwich Megisikwe!

Yes, an explanation point followed my name. Then in all caps:

OGEMA OSHKIBEWIKWE

Can you believe she would call me that? Chief woman among her helpers? Below that three initials were followed by three numbers:

I.H.B.105.

Indian Health Board, but what does the number mean? Was it the number assigned by the university for the class I helped her teach there: Great Lakes Indian Ethnobotany and Philosophy? Or was it the number of the room we met in? That large clean room near the parking lot on the jostling corner of 27ᵗʰ and Wisconsin Avenue, near the ma and pop diner, next to a row of taverns opening at 6 a.m., drunks lounged against traffic lights smoking pall malls, city bus belching dirt, March snow crusted into black rivers running down the cracked sidewalk into the sewer, street walkers hawking their young bodies between the flash and blast of red sirens.

Below this arranged with her attention to symmetry:

NASP   UWM

Native American Studies Program   University of Wisconsin-Milwaukee

Then in smaller letters near the bottom of the curving copper kettle:

December 1981

I was so young then hauling her cardboard boxes barely held together with black electrical tape. Tumbling out of them were jars of dried herbs, bottles of oils and tinctures, a coiled hot plate, an extension cord, zippered plastic bags labeled with the Anishinaabeg, the Latin, and the common names of those medicines she wanted me to help her bring back from the brink of forgetting.

She said without saying, Listen to what my ancestors knew. She wanted her students to stand up and sing prayers with their hands open and their hearts, she wanted their hearts.

She drew in white chalk on the blackboard: pistol, stamen, leaf pattern, floral pattern. I brewed the tea of the day from the plants we had harvested months earlier. (Kneeling at the edge of the swale, slapping mosquitos, knees damp, whispering gratitude as I picked the fragrant leaves of wild peppermint.) Pouring boiling water over the dried leaves, I recall the lake rippling beneath late afternoon thunderheads.

I was the only non-Native in that class of card-carrying tribal members from Potawatomi, Oneida, Stockbridge-Munsee, Red Cliff, Black River, Lac du Flambeau, Menominee, Lac Courte Oreilles.

Sometimes as she spoke I stared out the window into the potted street, dirty sheetrock, bricked-up windows, soggy newspaper, the hurried, harried social worker, the tired grandma with a kerchief tied below her chin, the hungry child throwing gravel at a stray dog. Two hundred years ago 27th Street was a ricing swamp, canoes gliding, muskrat feeding their young.

I close my eyes remembering what she taught me, everything.

Trilogy for the Atomic Physicist

I. The Doctors Had Given Up On Him

That's when he came to her.
I was there, I saw it.
Perhaps you could say
I was part of it, for I was the one
to collect the leaves
dry them in half shade
beneath the cedar tree
on the shed roof.
The one to heap the dried leaves
onto the concave stone
and light them. Steadying my breath
I blew spark into sweet smoke
filling the willow lodge.
Kneeling on earth
above the cattail mat where he lay
fever-glint in his eye
I touched the very places
my hand her eagle feather
our faces in the mist
of that green sacrifice.
Speaking the words I was taught
until he softened, and I stepped back,
that's when she emerged
barreling from the shadow
to slap the dying man
with a beaded bear paw.
Startled he shot up like an arrow
to live for another decade

II. He Asked Me to Help in a Good Way, the Right Way

Gathering it in
dark heart of the cave
sweet pollen breath
bee hive dance
the long dreaming
fish gleaming
love for this life

Gathering it in
the thrust, the contraction
belly low, heaving
hips breaking wide
the head of newborn
pushing, pushing
bearing down to birth
the dawn

Gathering it in
thunder clap, tree-splitting
lightning crack,
blackberry feast,
fog rising from the lake

Gathering it in
the wind howling
power of you now!

!

III. I Don't Want to Die

I was smart. They recruited me.
Brain like lightning. On fire.
We made the 20th century.
Splitting atoms our forté.
But it took energy.
We found it buried.
Yellow cake. Burned it.
Lit the cities. Built the armies.
Ten thousand warheads.
More than that.
Spilled bright tailings
into the mouths of deserts
into the blood of rivers
fish belly up
nine-fingered babies
goats with fused legs
poison cascading down
the canyons of jagged mountains.
I took ten thousand
painkillers, more than that.
You can kill people. Kill the land.
Kill hope. But you can't
kill pain. I know
what we did
made rich men richer
tore magnificent power
from the dirt, left
life-twisting destruction
millennia of waste.
So when I went
to the old Indian woman,
bile-yellow, liver dying

on my knees crying
and made the request for healing,
I believed nothing
but the wrenching
desire to live.When
the bear slapped me
its claws drew blood.
I deserved it.
I got up. Went right to work.
Helping the Navajo uranium miners.
What I do now. Every
breath of it. Giving back.

Healing

The life of a dreamer is not easy.
The dreams keep you awake.
                Essie Parrish, Pomo Indian Healer

Dream your hands
like twin suns rise
to flower in the heat,
each hand, a perfect
five-petalled blossom.

Dream your hands
emerge from wounded earth
like animal teeth or trees
cut for timber. You will
itch to reforest city lot.

Dream your fast hands swat flies
Your cool hands kill fever
Your piano hands kiss tusk
Your angry hands slap back
Your thieving hands steal time
Your dragon hands melt doubt
Your blind hands see
for the first time
the aura above my skin
And in the single motion of the flock
your hands swoop down to release me
from my cage of worry
flowing cloud hands
spilling over the whole thirsting Earth

Imagine what will be
when our fluttering, drumming
smoking, laboring, twitching
snapping, scarred, bitten, broken, pale
dark horse hands
thick with clay
shape dawn

Yes, dream.
Imitate your dreams
until you become them.

Bear Medicine

The trailhead to the Milky Way
is marked with a bear claw, for the bear
it is said, is a god, can calm the sick
lift fallen pine from wounded leg
eat the tender root to stave off starvation
gather berries in time of plague. The bear,
it is said, has sympathy for us,
helpless clawless fangless furless
clinging sucking small-boned ones,
and as long as we remember our place
to bend and honor and feed the good bear
in turn, bear will lead us to the cave
hold us when we cry a child's tears
feast and dance us to summer's end.
The bear, it is said, knows when to flee
scales the tree when enemies near.
Then at first ice crawls into dream
rising from the realm of the near-dead
to nurse the spring-born cub,
mother and cub, big dipper, little dipper
circling the North Star.
Is it possible that I remember
the sound of the sea,
salt slapping the wood hull
blue glacial melt, bear grease
smeared with wood ash to paint the cave wall
a ribbon of gray stone girdled in red, in white.
Winter dark parts the curtain of dream
we are curled and naked. I reach for you,
oh mothers of my mother's mother
oh splendid boy, bent old man
where do we keep the steps of the dance
on the map of the road to the dead?

Waterbird Medicine

for Bosque del Apache

The migrating flock rises
sandhill, great blue heron, snow geese
lift their long feathered wings
webbed talons skip edge of water
necks straining, beaks thrust forward
the racket, the pterodactyl cry of cranes
I stand, wingless, as they spiral upward
and my breath becomes a rung in the ladder
of ten billion animal breaths, each wing beat
rippling this air. I rise with them
into the trembling dawn
light flooding the land
and know now how
every human exhalation
feeds the body of green leaves.
Wind makes a passage for itself
makes a breath for itself
rushing through the hollow bone
of my flesh flute.
Whose breath blows
making music of me ?

The Oil Painter

We cannot heal ourselves until we heal the Earth.
We cannot heal the Earth until we heal ourselves.
       Rio de Janeiro Declaration, World Parliament of
       Indigenous Peoples, 1992

Snow clouds pony the gray mountain
Dried rosehips cling to the branch
Pockmarked ice on the north side
refuses to melt, and inside the soft cells
of her body: cadmium, thallium, lead,
the discarded ambition of empire
lodged against neuron, fatigue
dampening the will to live,
no more oil-rich paint
glossy against canvas, each stroke
of the brush lasting a thousand years,
what has been done is done,
beneath our flesh, a shadow
measured in micrograms
too late to learn
no safe level. In the long tired night
I rise up on one elbow
remembering a run
through the glen on a summer morning
her skin glistening with sweat
bright eyes smiling, me struggling
to keep up. What we do to the Earth
we do to ourselves. Is it too late
for her to say, *I am whole*
in this broken light.

The Hike

for N. G.

Sage first. Then sweetgrass.
Now tell me the history of your body.
Did you ever live beside the Platte River?
How old were you when you played
in the sludge at Point Beach Nuclear Plant?
Did you chow down the milk chocolate
from the dairy at Three Mile Island?
(enormous bovine eyes blinking at the sky)
Did you drink
unfiltered water from the
municipality of Milwaukee
the week the sewage backed up? Were
you nearby when the fires
raged above Los Alamos? How
many times did you cross
your heart and hope to
die, singing, ashes ashes
we all fall down? Did you
stumble in the subway
when the twin towers tumbled?
Did you witness the scrim
separating first class from the riff-raff
burst into flame? I cannot tell you
who the great-grandbaby of robber barons is,
or what peasants from which shtetl
carry the gene. You will not live
forever. The long sob of the blues
and the land-grab legacy of America
reminds us the carrier pigeons'
extinction could have been predicted

if anyone had been paying attention. This autumn
hike beneath gold aspens serves as
warning. Today, my friend, our hearts beat
hard, perspiration along our brows, your legs
pump like a twenty year old as we climb.
Leukemia is a word, but who can comprehend
such abstraction? A raven tips above
the rocky outcrop, daggers of sunlight
stab our eyes. We both stop
stand, breathe, wait, listen, live

before moving on

Make Your List

for A.K.

First white cedar, then trillium, moss, lichen
wild rose, St. Johnswort, bearberry
manzanita, eucalyptus and peppertree.
Maybe these plants, the way they grip
the soil, their edgeless reach
maybe if you memorize
their names. Maybe then. But there is also
the silver and turquoise
your mother collected in the '50s
on secret trips between Communist party members
traveling backroads between Los Angeles and Taos
to find others who believed healthcare
and housing were rights as fundamental as voting,
but the children, you among them,
wanted only dinosaur bones, chipped bits
of petrified forest, a glass jar of colored sand
so you could carry the painted desert in one hand.
You remember pink motel swimming pool,
ice cream melting into dust, your mother
squinting beneath a floppy hat,
unlit cigarette between cherry lips.
All of it matters. The strength
it took for her to flee the choking green
affluence of Illinois after your grandmother
was locked in the madhouse
for taking the tailor's scissors to her throat.
Add a pile of red beach stones,
black bear gazing through dense woods.
You cannot forget the story of how
your blonde Bauhaus artist mother,

met a Brooklyn Jew with a rebel streak
joined the Party, and raised a daughter
without knowing how to keep her
safe. You are the only one alive
carrying the memory of your life.
In it is the detail that will save you.

Freshman Essay on *Dia de los Muertos*

Day of the Dead
asters glow in the blast
of late afternoon sun
dried grasses bend in the wind
dark clouds double
over the crumpled volcanic ridge.
I stand before the freshman class
naked beneath my clothes
beneath my skin: bone
beneath rock: lava
the overwhelming presence
of what lives beneath.
Today families carry flowers
to the cemetery, discarded masks
litter the gutter: witch, vampire, ghost.
In the blackness between stars
in the dark within an egg
in the pupil of an eye
in the ache of ground
the dead recall the taste of spring.
Let us remember that
as we write

Teacher

My students, potent, beaten, explosive, ready,
are late to class again. I hear them
coming down the hall carried forward
by the endless tide of language. My door
is open, what enters the room
enters me, as in the dark lodge
when a single voice lifts
the red rock breaks open, certain
ceremonies never end.
We begin
with words and end with words
hurrying after the humming dark
undertow of the unanswerable.
We open the book to a page
to a title to a sentence
to a word to a letter
to a sound in the breath
of the body. We open our mouths.
We speak together.
I tell them. I tell myself.
Do not be afraid. Dive deeper.
To learn is to live.
Keep the door wide open.
We remain unfinished
for the teacher is
every one
every thing
every moment

The Medicine of Sacred Places

Places are beings. Surely, we know this.
Deer Medicine Rock. Sleeping Bear Dune.
Porcupine Mountain. Otter Creek. The last home
of wolf, fox, lynx, the stone shore
where bearberry grows. Go now.
Place your hands in the Earth. Breathe.
Let sunlight be your second skin.
Feel the soles of your feet root.
Dream at water's edge.
Crack your dark heart open.
Change
volcanic, meteoric, inchoate
means we live
here, appearing and disappearing
as the horizon is

Little Miami River

for Phyllis and Vernon

Twenty-five thousand years ago
right here, a glacier began to melt
torrents of stone flooded the frozen earth
and in the steep bed of a ravine
a new river formed.
At the bend in this river
beneath the horned owl's nest
I step into the icy current
pushing against my legs.
Last night my neighbor and his wife
refusing to be moved into a nursing home
tied plastic bags around their heads
turned on the machine from the Hemlock Society
ready to die. They held hands
quietly listening to the shush-shush of gas
and fell asleep. When he woke up
she was gone. I have been told
beneath this river another river
flows

Mountain Lion Medicine

for Kiki

Learn to live like this.
Here in the mud, in the ice melt
beside paw prints bigger than your palm
at the trailhead where the creek rushes
through a grove of white fir
stand in the breath-path of a panther.
Courage. At dawn the cougar
came down to drink
following her true thirst.

Scraping Buffalo Hide the Old Way

Flies circled the carcass soaked for four days
in a horse trough held down by belly-sized chunks
of pale pink rose quartz. Seven of us lift it
lace the hide onto the pine square frame.
One plays the flute, another smudges with sage.
We brace it against the trunk of a sycamore
and start scraping the rancid flesh.
Hours pass, morning becomes noon,
knees ache, flies bite, we sing
prayers until only the cicadas hum
then they too fall silent as the green wind
roars in from the west ferrying thunderheads.
One enormous bolt hammers down the power
we see its jagged white spear
splitting open the sky and race into the garage
singing *Buffalo Gals won't ya come out tonight*
come out tonight, come out tonight
pounding the freezer like a drum
dancing on the cement floor
while the fur on the hide in the storm
rises in the furious wind.
When storm ends, heat climbs
even as the sun drops
into the hills. Night floods
the eastern bank
covering us in a hot damp dark
slippery as the birth canal.
I cannot sleep
beneath the heavy hide
of this bison night
with each small knick
of the obsidian knife
letting in the light

Rose Medicine in Red Willow Basket

Circling the rose thicket I ponder its strategy
to protect beauty from being utterly
destroyed. I, too, have hidden thorns.
On Summer Solstice I fill a glass bowl
soak fresh-picked rose petals
in the long rays of that singular sunlight
making rose water for the year ahead.
Following frost I collect rosehips
to ward off flu with potent tea.
Circling the rose, the seasons circle me
I grow older. I have hidden so much
hoping to keep it safe. The danger now is clear.
Show up or disappear. What you know
will vanish like Spring snow.
Remember the red willow basket
full of stories, the gift I left
behind a stump in the swamp
not wanting anyone to know
what I was becoming
in the hush-hush twilight
before dawn birds sing.
While everyone slept
I made her bearberry tea,
and she told me stories.
Kneeling beside the fire,
blowing embers hotter
as the Dipper spun above
leaning out over the canoe edge
my body balanced to dip and lift
lake water for another cup
for these late night stories
disguised as laughter, as memory, as kindling.

Then gone into green shadow
until now, poking my head out.
I am almost the age she was
when I first arrived on that rocky shore.
Perhaps it is time.
Pick up the basket.

Ritual

When I moved to the high mesa
I realized some things must end,
the dark red secret, fecund as salt,
which I have celebrated
in spectacular monoprints
on morning sheets, my lunation,
shameless unbroken burden binding me
to mothers and daughters everywhere,
slows and finally ceases.

Light the candle.
I will again be new
at becoming

Glossary

Anishinaabeg: Anishinaabemowin (Ojibwe); literally, "The People," refers to the People of the Three Fires: Potawatomi, Ojibwe (Ojibway, Chippewa) and Odawa (Ottawa).

auto-de-fe: public ritual of punishment often involving torture and burning at the stake for heretics and apostates who challenged Catholic doctrine during the Spanish and Portuguese Inquisition, which also took place in Mexico, Peru, Brazil, and elsewhere.

beija-flor: Brazilian Portugeuse; hummingbird, literally kisses flower.

cascata: Portuguese; waterfall.

Dia de los Muertos: Spanish; Day of the Dead, important holiday celebrated on November 1 throughout Latin American, including New Mexico and Arizona.

fibre marche: French; Fiber Market, a major marketplace in Dakar, Senegal.

grand bu-bu: term for female clothing consisting of three matching pieces: a head cloth to wrap the hair, a loose long sleeve tunic, and a wrapped ankle-length skirt; common girls' and women's daily outfit in West Africa.

Halona:wa: Zuni (A:shiwi); the name for the central plaza at Zuni Pueblo.

kanji: Japanese script consisting of syllabic symbols.

mashkikikwe: Anishinaabemowin (Ojibwe); herbal medicine woman.

Megisikwe: spiritual name given to the author by Keewaydinoquay, has numerous translations or interpretations, including Sacred Shell Woman and Divine Guidance Woman, from the megis shell (cowrie).

miigwetchiwewin: Anishinaabemowin (Ojibwe); being in a state of gratitude, from miigwetch, thank you.

mishi megwich: Anishinaabemowin (Ojibwe); another spelling for thank you. Mishi, now more often shortened to Chi, means very much. Translation, Thank you very much.

ogema: Anishinaabemowin (Ojibwe); chief.

oshkibewis: Anishinaabemowin (Ojibwe); helper, singular; oshkibewig, plural; oshkibewikwe, female helper.

Sakura: Japanese celebration when the cherry trees are in full bloom in April.

shtetl: Yiddish; diminuitive form of shtot, town; a village in Central or Eastern Europe which had a large Jewish population until The Holocaust.

This book of poetry has been printed on acid-free paper.

∞

The typeface is Book Antiqua,
a varient of Palatino, which is based on the humanist
fonts of the Italian Renaissance, which mirror the letters
formed by a broad nib pen; this gives a calligraphic grace.
But where the Renaissance faces tend to use smaller letters
with longer vertical lines (ascenders and descenders)
with lighter strokes, Palatino has larger proportions,
and is considered to be a much easier to read typeface.